PRESIDENTS

JOHN F. KENNEDY

A MyReportLinks.com Book

Randy Schultz

MyReportLinks.com Books
an imprint of

Enslow Publishers, Inc.
Box 398, 40 Industrial Road
Berkeley Heights, NJ 07922
USA

*B
Kennedy's*

MyReportLinks.com Books, an imprint of Enslow Publishers, Inc.

Library of Congress Cataloging-in-Publication Data

Schultz, Randy.
    John F. Kennedy / Randy Schultz.
        p. cm. — (Presidents)
    Includes bibliographical references and index.
    Summary: Traces the life of the president who was assassinated in 1963.
Includes Internet links to Web sites, source documents, and
photographs related to John F. Kennedy.
    ISBN 0-7660-5012-2
    1. Kennedy, John F. (John Fitzgerald), 1917–1963—Juvenile literature. 2. Presidents—
United States—Biography—Juvenile literature. [1. Kennedy, John F. (John Fitzgerald), 1917–1963. 2.
Presidents.] I. Title. II. Series.
    E842.Z9S38 2002
    973.922'092—dc21
    [B]   2001006848

Printed in the United States of America

10 9 8 7 6 5 4 3 2 1

To Our Readers:
Through the purchase of this book, you and your library gain access to the Report Links that specifically
back up this book.
The Publisher will provide access to the Report Links that back up this book and will keep these Report
Links up to date on **www.myreportlinks.com** for three years from the book's first publication date.
We have done our best to make sure all Internet addresses in this book were active and appropriate when we
went to press. However, the author and the Publisher have no control over, and assume no liability for, the
material available on those Internet sites or on other Web sites they may link to.
The usage of the MyReportLinks.com Books Web site is subject to the terms and conditions stated on the
Usage Policy Statement on **www.myreportlinks.com.**
In the future, a password may be required to access the Report Links that back up this book. The password
is found on the bottom of page 4 of this book.
Any comments or suggestions can be sent by e-mail to comments@myreportlinks.com or to the address on
the back cover.

Photo Credits: Photo Credits: © Corel Corporation, pp. 1 (background), 3; Courtesy of
Corcoran.org, p. 25; Courtesy of JFK Library, pp. 1, 15, 16, 34, 41; Courtesy of MyReportLinks.com
Books, p. 4; Courtesy of the HistoryPlace.com, pp. 12, 29, 30, 31; Department of the Interior, p. 28;
Library of Congress, pp. 23, 42; Lyndon Baines Johnson Library, p. 38; National Park Service,
pp. 27, 33.

Cover Photo: © Corel Corporation (background); John F. Kennedy Library.

3065 2001436312

Contents

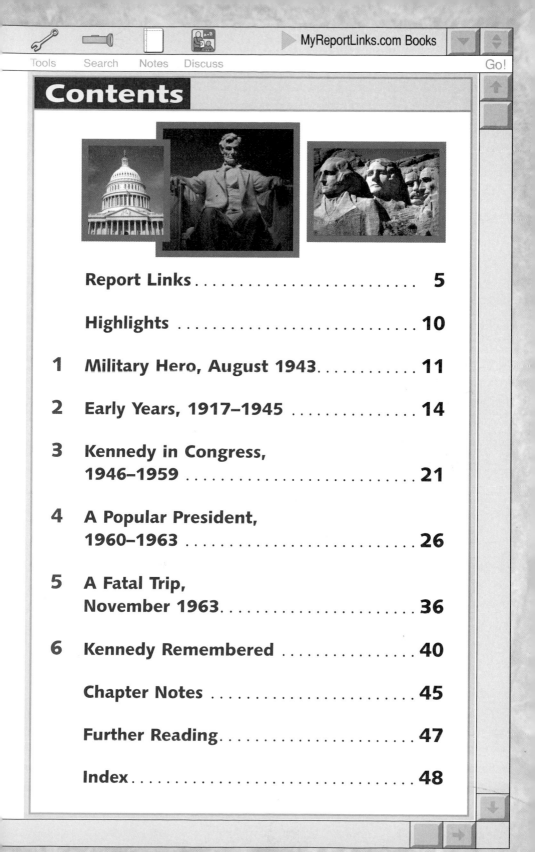

MyReportLinks.com Books
Great Books, Great Links, Great for Research!

MyReportLinks.com Books present the information you need to learn about your report subject. In addition, they show you where to go on the Internet for more information. The pre-evaluated Report Links that back up this book are kept up to date on **www.myreportlinks.com**. With the purchase of a MyReportLinks.com Books title, you and your library gain access to the Report Links that specifically back up that book. The Report Links save hours of research time and link to dozens—even hundreds—of Web sites, source documents, and photos related to your report topic.

Please see "To Our Readers" on the Copyright page for important information about this book, the MyReportLinks.com Books Web site, and the Report Links that back up this book.

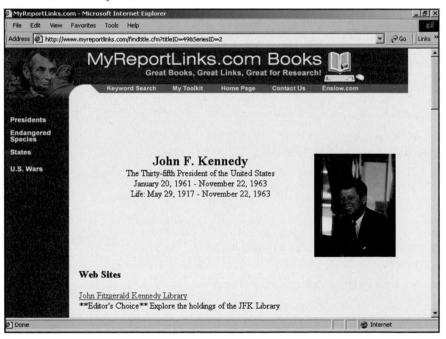

Access:

The Publisher will provide access to the Report Links that back up this book and will try to keep these Report Links up to date on our Web site for three years from the book's first publication date. Please enter **PKE1523** if asked for a password.

Report Links

The Internet sites described below can be accessed at
http://www.myreportlinks.com

▶**John Fitzgerald Kennedy Library**　　　　　　　*EDITOR'S CHOICE

At the JFK Library you will find a vast collection of speeches,
photographs, transcripts of televised debates, and JFK's biography.
You can also take a virtual tour of the museum.

Link to this Internet site from http://www.myreportlinks.com

▶**The Presidents: Kennedy**　　　　　　　　　　*EDITOR'S CHOICE

This PBS Web site traces John F. Kennedy's life from his early days to
his rise to the presidency. You will also find a collection of quotations,
speeches, letters, and highlights of his political career.

Link to this Internet site from http://www.myreportlinks.com

▶**John Fitzgerald Kennedy**　　　　　　　　　　*EDITOR'S CHOICE

At this Web site you will find facts and figures on John F. Kennedy.
You will also find links to Kennedy's presidential election results,
cabinet members, and historic documents.

Link to this Internet site from http://www.myreportlinks.com

▶**John F. Kennedy**　　　　　　　　　　　　　*EDITOR'S CHOICE

At this Web site you will find a comprehensive biography on John F.
Kennedy. Here you will learn about his personal life, the first lady, his
domestic and foreign affairs, and his legacy.

Link to this Internet site from http://www.myreportlinks.com

▶**John F. Kennedy Memorial Page**　　　　　　*EDITOR'S CHOICE

This site contains biographies about the Kennedys, a family tree, and
an elaborate collection of photographs and speeches.

Link to this Internet site from http://www.myreportlinks.com

▶**Kennedys**　　　　　　　　　　　　　　　*EDITOR'S CHOICE

This interactive Web site provides biographies of John F. Kennedy,
Jacqueline Kennedy, and John F. Kennedy, Jr. You will also find an
interactive time line that explores the family history of the Kennedys.

Link to this Internet site from http://www.myreportlinks.com

The Internet sites described below can be accessed at
http://www.myreportlinks.com

▶ **The :30 Second Candidate**
This PBS site explores the history of political commercials and debate. Here you will learn about the Nixon and Kennedy debate; the first presidential debate to be televised.

Link to this Internet site from http://www.myreportlinks.com

▶ **The American President: Episode 1: "Family Ties"**
This PBS site provides a brief explanation of John F. Kennedy's "Family Ties" and how they transformed the modern presidency. You will also find a historical document, an audio clip, and additional resources.

Link to this Internet site from http://www.myreportlinks.com

▶ **American Presidents: John F. Kennedy**
This Web site provides "Life Facts" and "Did you know?" trivia about John F. Kennedy. You can also read a letter written by JFK to Soviet Premier Nikita Khrushchev regarding the Cuban Missile Crisis.

Link to this Internet site from http://www.myreportlinks.com

▶ **Birthplace of John F. Kennedy: Home of the Boy Who Would Be President**
At this Web site you will learn about John F. Kennedy's birthplace in Brookline, Massachusetts. You will also find maps, additional reading material, and images of John F. Kennedy, his family, and home.

Link to this Internet site from http://www.myreportlinks.com

▶ **The Cold War Museum**
At the Cold War Museum you can explore events that occurred during the Cold War. Some topics covered are the U2 Incident, JFK's assassination, the Bay of Pigs invasion, the space race, and other events.

Link to this Internet site from http://www.myreportlinks.com

▶ **The Decision to Go to the Moon**
On May 25, 1961, John F. Kennedy announced to Congress his goal of sending an American to the moon. This site provides a history of the factors considered in sending a person to the moon and additional links to the history of space exploration.

Link to this Internet site from http://www.myreportlinks.com

Report Links

The Internet sites described below can be accessed at
http://www.myreportlinks.com

▶ **The History Place: John F. Kennedy Photo History**
This Web site provides a photographic history of John F. Kennedy's
early years, war years, political life, and presidency.

Link to this Internet site from http://www.myreportlinks.com

▶ **"I Do Solemnly Swear..."**
At this Web site you can experience John F. Kennedy's Inauguration
Day by browsing though documents, images, and sound recordings.

Link to this Internet site from http://www.myreportlinks.com

▶ **Index to Speeches by John F. Kennedy**
This site contains a collection of speeches given by John F. Kennedy
including his inaugural address, the Berlin Crisis, the Cuban Missile
Crisis, and his Civil Rights Message.

Link to this Internet site from http://www.myreportlinks.com

▶ **Jacqueline Kennedy: The White House Years**
This site explores Jacqueline Kennedy and the White House. Here
you will find an exhibit dedicated to Jacqueline Kennedy's influence
on fashion.

Link to this Internet site from http://www.myreportlinks.com

▶ **John F. Kennedy**
At this Web site you will find an overview of John F. Kennedy's life and
political career. You will also find Kennedy's inaugural address, quick
facts about his life, and a list of his cabinet members.

Link to this Internet site from http://www.myreportlinks.com

▶ **John F. Kennedy (1917–1963)**
At this site you will find a painting and photographs of John F.
Kennedy. Each image is accompanied with a brief note about JFK and
a description of the image.

Link to this Internet site from http://www.myreportlinks.com

→ The Internet sites described below can be accessed at
http://www.myreportlinks.com

John F. Kennedy (1917–1963)

The Smithsonian Archives of American Art holds a telegram from the Kennedys to poet Robert Richman. Also included are photos of Jacqueline Kennedy at the Whitney Museum, and a letter from her regarding the restoration of the White House.

Link to this Internet site from http://www.myreportlinks.com

John F. Kennedy: A Way With the People

In 1961, *Time* magazine presented John F. Kennedy with the Man of the Year award. At this site you can read the article written about him, which provides an assessment of Kennedy's administration.

Link to this Internet site from http://www.myreportlinks.com

Kennedy Family Album

This site contains a collection of photographs of the Kennedy family. Along with each photograph, you will find a brief description of the image and the year that it was taken.

Link to this Internet site from http://www.myreportlinks.com

Objects from the Presidency

At this site you will find objects related to President John F. Kennedy and a description of the era he lived in. You will also learn about the office of the presidency.

Link to this Internet site from http://www.myreportlinks.com

On This Day: Obituary of John Fitzgerald Kennedy

At the *New York Times* Learning Network Web site you will find a five part overview of John F. Kennedy's administration and links to the *New York Times* coverage of his assassination.

Link to this Internet site from http://www.myreportlinks.com

President John F. Kennedy

At this site you will find a biography of John F. Kennedy, where you will learn about his early life and rise to the presidency. You will also find an interesting fact, a quote, and links to major events in his administration.

Link to this Internet site from http://www.myreportlinks.com

Report Links

The Internet sites described below can be accessed at
http://www.myreportlinks.com

▶ **The President John F. Kennedy Assassination Records Collection**
At this Web site you will find a vast collection of documents relating to John F. Kennedy's assassination, such as the Warren Commission's report.

Link to this Internet site from http://www.myreportlinks.com

▶ **President John F. Kennedy Was Shot in Dallas, Texas**
America's Story from America's Library, a Library of Congress Web site, provides a brief overview of John F. Kennedy's assassination on November 22, 1963.

Link to this Internet site from http://www.myreportlinks.com

▶ **The Presidential Election of 1960**
The Library of Congress Learning Page offers an overview of the Election of 1960 and explores the presidential elections from the past and present. Here you will learn how the Election of 1960 is thought to have changed American politics.

Link to this Internet site from http://www.myreportlinks.com

▶ **A Timeline of the American Civil Rights Movement**
Here you will find an overview of important civil rights cases and protests, such as *Brown* vs. *the Board of Education* and the Montgomery Bus Boycott.

Link to this Internet site from http://www.myreportlinks.com

▶ **The White House: Jacqueline Lee Bouvier Kennedy**
The official White House Web site holds the biography of Jacqueline Lee Bouvier Kennedy. Here you will learn about her life and the national attention she brought to the arts.

Link to this Internet site from http://www.myreportlinks.com

▶ **The White House: John Kennedy**
The official White House Web site holds a biography of John F. Kennedy. Here you will learn about his accomplishments as president, and his assassination.

Link to this Internet site from http://www.myreportlinks.com

Highlights

1917—*May 29:* John Fitzgerald Kennedy is born at home, in Brookline, Massachusetts. He is the first president born in the twentieth century.

1936—Attends Harvard University.

1940—Attends Stanford Business School. Senior thesis published as *Why England Slept,* achieves wide acceptance.

1941—Begins four-year service in the Navy.

1947—Elected to the United States House of Representatives.

1953—*Sep. 12:* Marries Jacqueline L. Bouvier.

—Elected to the United States Senate.

1956—Writes the collective biography *Profiles in Courage*, for which he is awarded the Pulitzer Prize.

1960—*Nov. 8:* Elected president.

1961—*Jan. 20:* Inaugurated president, delivering the famous lines, "Ask not what your country can do for you—ask what you can do for your country . . . ."

—*March 1:* Creates the Peace Corps by executive order.

—*April 17–20:* Accepts responsibility for failure of Bay of Pigs Invasion of Cuba.

—*May:* Alan B. Shepard, Jr., becomes the first American in space, fulfilling Kennedy's objective.

—*Aug.:* Signs charter for the Alliance for Progress.

1962—*Oct.:* Negotiates Cuban Missile Crisis.

1963—*June:* Makes impassioned speech at the Berlin Wall.

—*Oct.:* Signs the Limited Nuclear Test Ban Treaty with Great Britain and the Soviet Union.

—*Nov. 22, 12:30 P.M.:* Assassinated in Dallas, Texas, by Lee Harvey Oswald.

—*Nov. 24:* Lee Harvey Oswald is murdered by Dallas nightclub owner Jack Ruby.

1964—Warren Commission, headed by Supreme Court Chief Justice Earl Warren, finds that Oswald had acted alone in killing Kennedy, but controversy surrounding the killing continues.

Military Hero, August 1943

When Japan attacked Pearl Harbor, Hawaii, on the morning of December 7, 1941, the United States was forced to enter World War II. John F. Kennedy, who had enlisted in the Navy just a few months earlier, was assigned to patrol torpedo (PT) boat training.

As the war went on, Kennedy was eventually promoted to the rank of lieutenant junior grade. In March 1943, he was given command of his own torpedo boat, *PT–109*, in the South Pacific. For weeks *PT–109*, along with many other PT boats, patrolled the waters in search of enemy destroyers operated by the Japanese.

In the early morning hours of August 2, 1943, *PT–109* and fourteen other PT boats were patrolling the waters of the Solomon Islands, just northeast of Australia. They had been assigned to block Japanese destroyers from slipping through the area to drop off supplies on islands occupied by Japanese troops.[1]

As the fifteen PT boats spread out, a few, including *PT–109*, began drifting farther out to sea than they realized. Throughout the night the PT boats were under fire, both from land and sea, by the Japanese.

Since *PT–109* had drifted away from the other ships, it was not under fire. After awhile, the gunfire stopped. The night was quiet. At about 2:00 A.M., *PT–109* was joined by *PT–157* and *PT–169*. All three began moving quietly up the Blackett Strait.

They were just west of New Georgia Island at around 2:30 A.M., when a cry went up from the Kennedy boat:

"Ship at two o'clock."[2] That meant an enemy was coming from the northeast.

The "ship" was the Japanese destroyer *Amagiri*. It was bearing down right on top of Kennedy and the rest of his *PT–109* crew. The destroyer, under the command of Kohei Hanami, sliced through *PT–109* within seconds.[3]

The force of the hit sent Kennedy, along with the rest of his crew, flying into the water. The *Amagiri* continued on its way into the Pacific, leaving *PT–109* in flames.

Two of *PT–109*'s crew members were killed instantly. Kennedy and the others were injured. Kennedy and ten survivors clung to the wreckage of their boat.

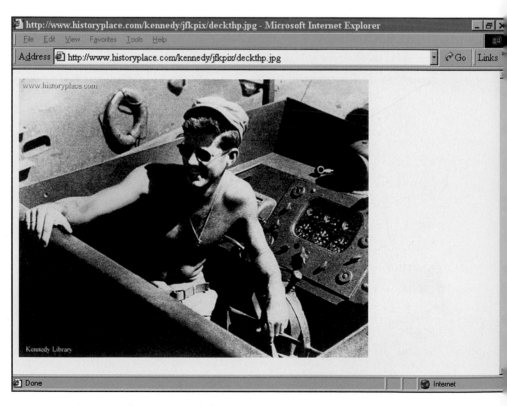

http://www.historyplace.com/kennedy/jfkpix/deckthp.jpg - Microsoft Internet Explorer

File Edit View Favorites Tools Help

Address http://www.historyplace.com/kennedy/jfkpix/deckthp.jpg   Go   Links

www.historyplace.com

Kennedy Library

Done   Internet

▲ Kennedy was awarded the Navy and Marine Corps Medal for his courage and bravery in the terrible ordeal in the South Pacific.

By daylight, Kennedy had spotted a small island. Nine of his crew members made a makeshift raft out of scrap material left afloat from *PT–109*. Kennedy tried to help Engineer Patrick McMahon, who had been seriously burned in the collision. Kennedy took two straps from the life jacket McMahon was wearing. He tied the straps together to form a harness, then took the strap between his teeth and began swimming. Despite an injured back, Kennedy pulled the wounded sailor along.[4]

After about five hours of swimming, an exhausted Kennedy made it to the beach on the small island of Nauru with the rest of the surviving crew. On the fourth day two island natives arrived in a canoe. He took a coconut and carved the message, "Native knows Posit [position], Nauru Isl, he can pilot, 11 alive, need small boat."[5]

The natives took the coconut message and went to get help. The following day, they returned with a letter from Lieutenant A. R. Evans, an Australian coastwatcher.

On August 7, Kennedy and his crew were rescued. Kennedy received the Navy and Marine Corps Medal for his heroism and leadership. He was also awarded the Purple Heart, which is given to those wounded in combat.

By December 1943, Lieutenant Kennedy returned to the United States suffering from malaria and an injured back. He spent the rest of his naval service time as an instructor or as a patient in several military hospitals getting treatment for his back injury.[6]

Kennedy's heroic actions would become legendary. It seemed like just the right springboard the young man would need as he began looking toward a career in politics.

Early Years, 1917–1945

John Fitzgerald Kennedy was born on May 29, 1917, in Brookline, Massachusetts, a suburb of Boston. "Jack," as he would become known through his early years, was the second of nine children born to Joseph P. and Rose Fitzgerald Kennedy.

Kennedy was born with one leg longer than the other. But even worse, he was born with a poor immune system.[1] The infant Kennedy had an adrenal deficiency. Prayers were said on the day he was born in hopes that he would survive.

The situation was so serious that a priest administered to Kennedy the sacrament known as "anointing of the sick." Roman Catholic priests only perform this rite if a person is very elderly, seriously ill, or is likely to die from something such as an accident. The priest prays for the forgiveness of the person's sins and for the person's recovery. This would be the first of five times that Kennedy would receive this sacrament.

Fortunately, baby Jack survived. Still, he continued to be a frail and sickly child, with health problems through much of his life. It was said at the time that Kennedy had the will to live. He also had the will to be great.[2]

▶ Joseph Kennedy, Sr.

Jack's father was one of the wealthiest men in the United States. His fortune was estimated at $250 million. He had made his money through a variety of ventures including shipbuilding, moviemaking, real estate, and banking.

Under President Franklin D. Roosevelt, Joe Kennedy served as chairman of the U.S. Maritime Commission, chairman of the U.S. Securities and Exchange Commission, and ambassador to Great Britain. Joseph P. Kennedy even considered running for president at one time.[3]

Jack's mother, Rose Kennedy, was the daughter of a former mayor of Boston, John Francis "Honey Fitz" Fitzgerald. Rose grew up to be highly religious, very independent, worldly, and extremely interested in politics.

Throughout his early years, Jack found himself in the shadow of his older brother, Joseph, Jr. There always seemed to be a rivalry between them. As the family grew,

http://www.jfklibrary.org/images/kfc2476p.jpg - Microsoft Internet Explorer

File   Edit   View   Favorites   Tools   Help

Address   http://www.jfklibrary.org/images/kfc2476p.jpg   Go   Links

Done   Internet

▲ Jack's father, Joseph Kennedy, Sr., was a very wealthy and prominent man.

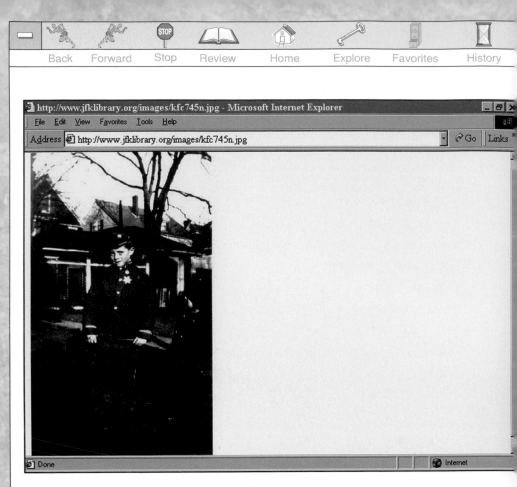

▲ *John F. Kennedy at age eight.*

the Kennedy children were highly competitive among themselves, thanks in part to their father's influence. At the same time, the children also developed a strong sense of loyalty to one another.

When Jack was young, the Kennedy family moved from Brookline to New York City. This way, Joe Kennedy, Sr., could be closer to his business dealings. After completing the sixth grade in the Bronxville, New York, public schools, thirteen-year-old Jack was sent to Canterbury School in New Milford, Connecticut. This was a Roman Catholic private school. Later Jack was sent to Choate, a nonreligious private school in Wallingford, Connecticut.

School Days

While a student at Choate, Jack wrote home: "If it were not for Latin, I would probably lead the lower school. But I am flunking that by 10 points." His father responded, encouraging young Jack to do his best: "After long experience in sizing up people I definitely know you have the goods and you can go a long way . . . I will not be disappointed if you don't turn out to be a real genius, but I think that you can be a really worthwhile citizen with good judgement and good understanding."[4]

Jack was also sick while at Choate. Once he became so ill that he could not be moved from his room. He spent much of his time reading books and newspapers, and he developed a love for history.

In 1935, Jack graduated from Choate. He was ranked sixty-fourth in a class of 112, but he was voted "most likely to succeed" by his classmates. Kennedy received the vote because of the campaigning he had done for it. Many have said that this was the first political campaign of Jack Kennedy's life.

From Choate it was on to the London School of Economics. Again, he was following in the footsteps of older brother, Joe.

Kennedy's stay at the school was shortened when he again became seriously ill. That illness was later identified as Addison's disease, a disease that attacks the adrenal glands, which are located on top of the kidneys. Kennedy eventually returned home to Massachusetts. Instead of enrolling in Harvard University like his father and older brother had, Jack Kennedy decided to enter Princeton University in New Jersey. A recurrence of his earlier illness forced him to withdraw from Princeton.

Following a recuperation period, Kennedy then decided to enter Harvard in 1936. During his first two years at Harvard, Kennedy received average grades. In the fall of 1937, he suffered a back injury while playing football with family members. It was the beginning of lifelong back problems for him. He was also hospitalized for blood disorders around that time.

Kennedy's junior year at Harvard was a turning point for him. It was the fall of 1938, and World War II had not yet begun. Kennedy decided to spend part of the year traveling across Europe. In each country he toured, he saw evidence of the spread of the ideas put forth by Adolf Hitler and the Nazi Party. Every place he went Kennedy saw people preparing for the outbreak of war. Every place, that is, except England.

▶ Respected Scholar

The trip to Europe inspired Kennedy to write an insightful senior paper, "Appeasement at Munich." Written in the autumn of 1939, it dealt with England's failure to prepare for the upcoming war as a response to the challenge of Hitler.

The paper was so well received that Kennedy rewrote it in 1940 to be published as the book *Why England Slept*. It became an instant best-seller.

Kennedy graduated with honors from Harvard in the spring of 1940. Following graduation from Harvard, Kennedy attended Stanford University for a short time. He then left Stanford to tour South America.

When he returned to the United States, Kennedy attempted to enter the Army Officer Candidate School. Unfortunately, he failed the physical. He was also rejected from the U.S. Navy for the same reasons.

Believing that war was just around the corner for the United States, Kennedy spent several months exercising to strengthen his back. He then reapplied for the Navy and was commissioned as an ensign in September 1941. Ensign is a rank above a chief warrant officer and below lieutenant junior grade.

The United States entered World War II when Japan bombed Pearl Harbor on December 7, 1941. In late 1942, Kennedy was assigned to a patrol torpedo boat squadron. By March 1943, Lieutenant Kennedy was in command of the *PT–109*. It was about five months later when Kennedy's boat was attacked.

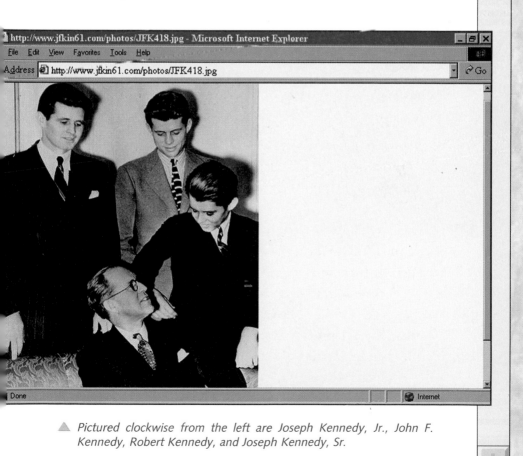

http://www.jfkin61.com/photos/JFK418.jpg - Microsoft Internet Explorer

File Edit View Favorites Tools Help

Address http://www.jfkin61.com/photos/JFK418.jpg Go

Done   Internet

▲ *Pictured clockwise from the left are Joseph Kennedy, Jr., John F. Kennedy, Robert Kennedy, and Joseph Kennedy, Sr.*

Kennedy was eventually sent back to the United States because of malaria and back problems that had been aggravated by sea duty. He had a spinal operation and spent over a year recovering in the hospital.

In August 1944, while still in the hospital, Kennedy received the bad news that his older brother, Joe, Jr., a Navy pilot, had been killed. His plane went down while on a secret bombing mission over Belgium. By 1945, Jack Kennedy had retired from the Navy. While resting in the hospital, Jack had remembered a story that had been told to him by other family members about Joe, Jr.

On the day that Joe, Jr., had been born, "Honey Fitz" Fitzgerald had said that the boy would grow up someday to be the president of the United States.[5] Now that Joe, Jr., was dead, Jack knew in his heart that he would have to take over for his fallen brother. Kennedy would later explain that he entered politics "because Joe died."[6] His older brother had been counted on as the member of the family most likely to go into politics.

Jack now took it upon himself to begin a career as a public servant, as Joe, Jr., would have done.

Chapter 3

Kennedy in Congress, 1946–1959

Following the end of World War II in 1945, Jack Kennedy completed his tour of military duty. Next, he decided to try his hand at newspaper reporting. Many members of Kennedy's family thought he would become a reporter or a teacher. He worked for awhile for the Hearst International News Service. After covering a couple of major world events, Kennedy decided to go into politics.

http://www.jfkin61.com/photos/JFK520.jpg - Microsoft Internet Explorer

File   Edit   View   Favorites   Tools   Help

Address http://www.jfkin61.com/photos/JFK520.jpg

Go to "http://www.jfkin61.com/photos/JFK520.jpg"

Done   Internet

▲ As a senator and later as president, Kennedy worked closely with his brother Bobby.

Kennedy began his political career in 1946 at his father's urging. A seat in the strongly Democratic 11th Congressional District of Massachusetts opened up. Ten candidates, including Kennedy, entered the Democratic primary race.

Many of Kennedy's brothers and sisters, as well as his mother, campaigned for him. With the support of his family, Jack Kennedy won the primary. He received twice as many votes as his nearest opponent. Kennedy then went on to easily defeat his Republican opponent.

"Just as I went into politics because Joe died, if anything happens to me tomorrow, my brother Bobby would run for my seat in the Senate," Jack would say later when he was a U.S. senator. "And if Bobby died, Teddy would take over for him."[1]

Kennedy was just twenty-nine years old when he took his seat in Congress in 1947. Later that year, he once again became seriously ill. Doctors discovered that Kennedy was again suffering from a malfunction of the adrenal glands.[2] Doctors prescribed a medicine that Kennedy would take daily to control the ailment. Kennedy would take the medicine for the rest of his life.

While serving in Congress, Kennedy worked hard for any bill that would help the people of Massachusetts. He voted for most of the social welfare programs of President Harry S Truman.

▶ Kennedy Runs for the Senate

Kennedy was reelected to Congress again in 1948 and 1950. By his second term in the House of Representatives, he realized that he wanted to climb higher on the political ladder. By 1952, he had decided to run for U.S. senator from Massachusetts.

Kennedy ran against a Republican, Senator Henry Cabot Lodge, Jr., a very popular politician in the state. Many felt that Lodge, the incumbent, would easily win the election.

Again, Kennedy's family, including brothers, sisters, sisters-in-law, brothers-in-law and his mother, got out and campaigned for him. His father, Joe, Sr., managed the campaign.

Dwight D. Eisenhower, the Republican candidate for president that year, carried Massachusetts by 208,800 votes. Surprisingly,

▲ *President Dwight D. Eisenhower.*

though, Kennedy defeated Lodge by more than seventy thousand votes. Because of his victory, Kennedy became a senator and his state's most well-known Democrat.

▶ Marriage and Family

In 1951, Jack Kennedy met his future wife, Jacqueline "Jackie" Lee Bouvier, at a dinner party in Washington, D.C. She was the daughter of wealthy Wall Street broker John V. Bouvier III. Kennedy courted her during his campaign for the Senate.

During this time, Jackie was working as a reporter for a Washington newspaper, and they soon became engaged. On September 12, 1953, the two were married at Newport, Rhode Island.

At first, the Kennedys had some trouble starting their family. A daughter was stillborn on August 23, 1956, and

was unnamed. Another daughter, Caroline Bouvier, was born on November 27, 1957. A son, John F., Jr., would be born on November 25, 1960. Another son, Patrick Bouvier, would be born prematurely on August 7, 1963. He died two days later.

Nearly a Vice President

In 1956, Kennedy received quite a bit of national exposure at the Democratic National Convention. The relatively unknown Kennedy was nearly chosen over Senator Estes Kefauver of Tennessee for the vice presidential nomination.

Kennedy the Senator

As a senator, Kennedy devoted a great deal of his time to helping with the problems in Massachusetts, as well as the rest of New England. He sponsored bills to help local industries such as fishing, textile manufacturing, and watchmaking. Kennedy served on the Senate Labor Committee and the Government Operations Committee.

Kennedy's health became an issue. Throughout his years as a congressman, Jack continued to suffer from back problems. By 1954, he was on crutches and required surgery. Two operations were performed, one in 1954 and the other in 1955. Both times complications occurred from surgery and Kennedy was near death.

Fortunately, Kennedy survived. During his long recovery, Kennedy had plenty of time to focus on his writing. He wrote a book on the subject of political courage called *Profiles In Courage*. Published in 1956, the text profiled eight United States senators who put principles above politics. It was awarded the Pulitzer Prize for Biography the following year.

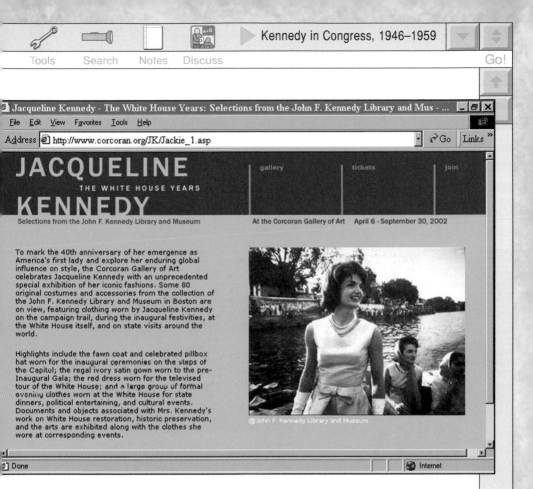

JACQUELINE
THE WHITE HOUSE YEARS
KENNEDY

Selections from the John F. Kennedy Library and Museum   At the Corcoran Gallery of Art   April 6 - September 30, 2002

gallery   tickets   join

To mark the 40th anniversary of her emergence as America's first lady and explore her enduring global influence on style, the Corcoran Gallery of Art celebrates Jacqueline Kennedy with an unprecedented special exhibition of her iconic fashions. Some 80 original costumes and accessories from the collection of the John F. Kennedy Library and Museum in Boston are on view, featuring clothing worn by Jacqueline Kennedy on the campaign trail, during the inaugural festivities, at the White House itself, and on state visits around the world.

Highlights include the fawn coat and celebrated pillbox hat worn for the inaugural ceremonies on the steps of the Capitol; the regal ivory satin gown worn to the pre-Inaugural Gala; the red dress worn for the televised tour of the White House; and a large group of formal evening clothes worn at the White House for state dinners, political entertaining, and cultural events. Documents and objects associated with Mrs. Kennedy's work on White House restoration, historic preservation, and the arts are exhibited along with the clothes she wore at corresponding events.

@John F. Kennedy Library and Museum

John F. Kennedy married Jacqueline Bouvier on September 12, 1953. Jackie is perhaps most revered for her calm composure following her husband's death.

In 1957, Kennedy became a member of the Senate Foreign Relations Committee, a key assignment in Congress. He was critical of the Republicans' foreign policy. Instead, Kennedy supported a program of increased aid to underdeveloped countries.

Kennedy ran again for Senate in 1958. This time he defeated his Republican opponent in a landslide. Now Kennedy was a leading candidate for the 1960 Democratic presidential nomination.

Chapter 4 ▶

A Popular President, 1960–1963

While Jack Kennedy may have felt that he had a shot at the presidency in 1960, there were many other Americans who did not. There were many Democratic leaders who felt that Kennedy was too young. Others felt that Kennedy's Roman Catholic religion would work against him. The only other Roman Catholic ever nominated for president was Alfred E. Smith, who was badly defeated in 1928 by Herbert Hoover. Some voters were concerned that as a Roman Catholic, Kennedy might let the Pope influence some of his decisions.

▶ Kennedy Announces His Candidacy

Despite the opposition to his age and religion, Kennedy announced his candidacy for president in January 1960. He won presidential primaries in New Hampshire, Wisconsin, Indiana, West Virginia, Delaware, Nebraska, and Oregon.

By the time Kennedy reached the 1960 Democratic National Convention in Los Angeles, he was practically assured of the presidential nomination. He was nominated on the first ballot. Kennedy then chose Senator Lyndon B. Johnson as his vice presidential running mate.

The Republicans chose Vice President Richard M. Nixon to run against Kennedy. Henry Cabot Lodge, Jr., Kennedy's major opponent during his Senate days, was chosen as the Republican vice presidential candidate.

Kennedy–Nixon Debates

The 1960 campaign turned out to be one of the most hard-fought races in United States history. Kennedy and Nixon campaigned throughout the country. Thanks to several key television debates between the two candidates, Kennedy dispelled the notion that he was too young and inexperienced to run the country. The debates also marked the first time that presidential candidates had argued campaign issues face-to-face on television. Many felt that Kennedy appeared much more comfortable than Nixon during the debates. This definitely helped his bid for election.[1]

In the end, Kennedy defeated Nixon by fewer than 115,000 popular votes. He clearly won the majority of votes in the electoral college. Kennedy received 303 electoral votes to Nixon's 219. Virginia senator, Harry F. Byrd, received the other 15 electoral votes.

▲ The televised debates of 1960 between Kennedy and Nixon were the first in history.

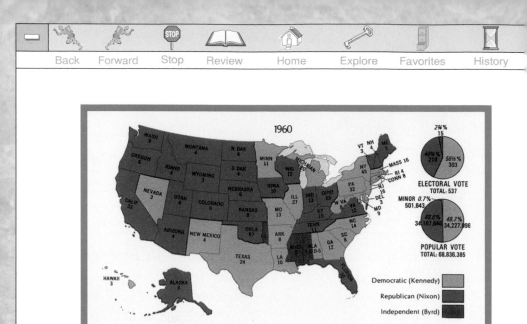

▲ *This map shows the results of the presidential election of 1960.*

▶ President Kennedy

On January 20, 1961, John F. Kennedy was sworn in as the thirty-fifth president of the United States. At forty-three, he was the youngest person ever elected to the office. Kennedy was also the first United States president born in the twentieth century. In his inaugural address, Kennedy spoke to the youth of the country:

> Let every nation know, whether it wishes us well or ill, that we shall pay any price, bear any burden, meet any hardship, support any friend, oppose any foe to assure the survival and the success of liberty.

> . . . In the long history of the world, only a few generations have been granted the role of defending freedom in its hour of maximum danger. I do not shrink from this responsibility; I welcome it. I do not believe that any of us would exchange places with any other people or any other generation. The energy, the faith, the devotion which we bring to this endeavor will light our country and all who serve it, and the glow from that fire can truly light the world.

And so, my fellow Americans, ask not what your country can do for you; ask what you can do for your country . . ."[2]

The New Frontier

Just as Kennedy had campaigned for a "New Frontier," he began his presidential programs using the same idea. One of the his greatest accomplishments was the formation of the U.S. Peace Corps in 1961. The corps was designed to send thousands of Americans abroad to help people in poorer nations raise their standard of living.

The new president also fought against the United States Steel Corporation when they tried to raise steel

http://www.historyplace.com/kennedy/jfkpix/oaththp.jpg - Microsoft Internet Explorer

File   Edit   View   Favorites   Tools   Help

Address http://www.historyplace.com/kennedy/jfkpix/oaththp.jpg   Go   Links

Done   Internet

▲ On January 20, 1961, Kennedy was sworn in as president of the United States. He was the youngest person ever elected president.

prices by six dollars a ton. Kennedy put down the move, saying it was too much, and the companies canceled the raise.

Right after he took office, Kennedy set a goal of landing a man on the moon by the end of the 1960s. As a result, a greater emphasis was put on improving NASA, the nation's space agency. On May 6, 1961, Alan B. Shepard, Jr., became the first American in space when he made his suborbital flight. On February 20, 1962, John H. Glenn, Jr., became the first American to orbit the earth. Although Kennedy would not witness it, in 1969, U.S. astronaut Neil Armstrong became the first man to set foot on the moon.

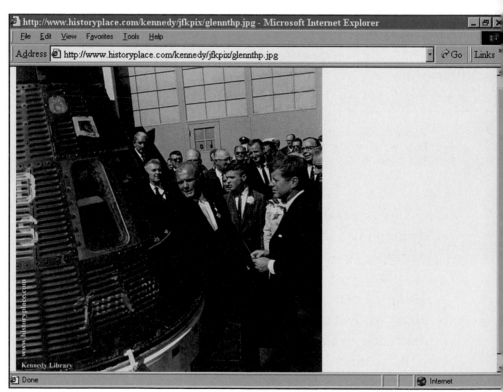

http://www.historyplace.com/kennedy/jfkpix/glennthp.jpg - Microsoft Internet Explorer

File   Edit   View   Favorites   Tools   Help

Address   http://www.historyplace.com/kennedy/jfkpix/glennthp.jpg   Go   Links

www.historyplace.com
Kennedy Library

Done   Internet

▲ Astronaut John Glenn shows Kennedy the space capsule in which he traveled into orbit and circled the earth three times.

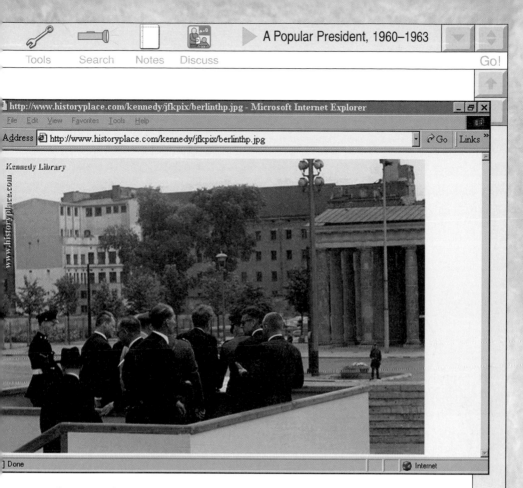

http://www.historyplace.com/kennedy/jfkpix/berlinthp.jpg - Microsoft Internet Explorer

File   Edit   View   Favorites   Tools   Help

Address http://www.historyplace.com/kennedy/jfkpix/berlinthp.jpg   Go   Links

Kennedy Library

www.historyplace.com

Done   Internet

▲ *During his trip to Germany in 1963, Kennedy visited the Berlin Wall. This photo shows the president looking across at a guard from East Germany.*

Civil rights issues came to light under the Kennedy administration. Riots had broken out at the University of Mississippi when an African-American student named James H. Meredith had tried to register for classes at the all-white school. On September 30, 1962, Kennedy sent federal marshals to restore order. Meredith was allowed to register and eventually graduated.

By 1963, Kennedy had firmly committed his administration to the cause of civil rights. The president sent a message to Congress in June of that year. In that message, he proposed the most comprehensive civil rights

bill since the period following the Civil War nearly one hundred years earlier. That bill was passed shortly after Kennedy's death.

Other legislative proposals made by Kennedy included providing hospital care for the aged through social security and giving federal aid to public schools. Again, both passed shortly after Kennedy was killed.

▶ International Affairs

In 1961, the United States established the Alliance for Progress, a ten-year program designed to send economic aid to Latin American countries that agreed to begin democratic reforms.

Toward the end of his administration, President Eisenhower gave approval for a Central Intelligence Agency (CIA) program to train Cuban exiles to invade Cuba. In April 1961, Kennedy secretly gave permission to launch the invasion. The purpose of the invasion was to spark an uprising in Cuba and overthrow the Communist government led by Fidel Castro. The invasion, which began at the Bay of Pigs, was a complete failure. The president took full responsibility but was humiliated by the exiles' defeat.

In August 1961, East German Communists put up a wall that separated East and West Berlin in Germany. The Communists wanted to stop East Germans from escaping to the west side of Berlin, which was controlled by West Germany. Cold War tensions rose when Kennedy sent more American troops into Germany. The crisis eventually eased after a military standoff at the border.

In October 1962, the United States almost went to war with the Soviet Union for a different reason. The United States found out that the Soviet Union was secretly placing

▲ *Despite Kennedy's talks with Khrushchev in Vienna in June 1961, the United States discovered that the Soviet Union was secretly placing ballistic missiles in Cuba.*

ballistic missiles in Cuba. The president immediately ordered a naval blockade of Cuba. United States warships surrounded the island, preventing other ships from carrying arms or oil into Cuba. Kennedy's goal was to remove all offensive weapons from Cuba.

Both the United States and Soviet Union put their armed forces on special alert. Many believed that the world was on the brink of a nuclear war. War was avoided when Premier Nikita S. Khrushchev of the Soviet Union agreed to remove the weapons from Cuba. Kennedy then lifted the blockade.

Following that American-Soviet confrontation, Kennedy wanted to bring about a lessening of international tension. What resulted was the Limited Nuclear Test Ban Treaty initiated by the United States, Soviet Union, and Great Britain. The treaty, signed on July 25, 1963, was designed to forbid the testing of nuclear weapons in the atmosphere, in space, and under water. Eventually more than one hundred nations would sign the treaty.

▶ Life with the Kennedy Family

President Kennedy and his young family brought an aura of youthfulness to the White House. Caroline and John,

MRBM LAUNCH SITE 2
SAN CRISTOBAL
1 NOVEMBER 1962

FUEL TRAILERS

MISSILE-READY TENT

FORMER LAUNCH POSITIONS

FORMER LOCATION OF MISSILE-READY TENTS

▲ *During his first two years as president, Kennedy dealt with many sensitive issues, such as the Cuban Missile Crisis in 1962. This photo shows where some of the Soviet missiles in Cuba were located.*

Jr., were the youngest children of a president to live in the White House in more than sixty years.

Jacqueline Kennedy was a trendsetter with her stylish clothes and hairstyles. She went with her husband to Europe and was met by huge crowds of fans. The president once said at a luncheon in Paris, France, "I am the man who accompanied Jacqueline Kennedy to Paris."[3]

Mrs. Kennedy became even more popular when she redecorated the White House. She was able to gather furnishings from past presidents. Because of her collections, the White House became an even more popular tourist attraction. In the years before the Kennedy White House, the interior of the building had fallen into disrepair.

The president also gave recognition to the creative arts, especially in the fields of music and entertainment. Many artists were invited to the White House to perform during the Kennedy administration.

▶ Kennedy Looking Ahead

By the middle of 1963, President Kennedy was looking ahead to the following election year. He felt that he had a good chance of winning, but he would soon have to begin campaigning.

Kennedy knew he would have to win over opposition to him in the state of Texas. He planned to visit Texas in November. It would be one of the most memorable presidential trips in United States history.

Chapter 5

A Fatal Trip, November 1963

As part of the campaign trail, a trip to Texas was planned in November 1963. Texas was Vice President Lyndon B. Johnson's home state. The chief purpose of the trip was to heal a split in the Texas Democratic Party before the 1964 presidential campaign got underway.[1] Dallas, known as a center for people who strongly opposed the Kennedy administration, was a key stop.

Kennedy flew to Texas, accompanied by his wife, the vice president, and Mrs. Johnson. *Air Force One* left Washington, D.C., on Thursday, November 21, and flew to San Antonio, Houston, and Fort Worth.

As part of the trip, Kennedy dedicated four new buildings at the USAF School of Aerospace Medicine at Brooks Air Force Base and had dinner in Houston.

On the morning of November 22, the Kennedys and Johnsons attended a breakfast in Forth Worth. The group was scheduled to be at a luncheon at noon in Dallas.

▶ Trip to Dallas

The plans in Dallas called for the president, Mrs. Kennedy, the Johnsons, and others to travel in a motorcade through the streets of the city. Their final destination was supposed to be the Dallas Trade Mart.

Kennedy rode in an open limousine. The president sat in the back seat, with his wife, Jacqueline, sitting next to him on his left. In front of him, in a "jump" seat on the right side of the car, sat Texas Governor John B. Connally.

Mrs. Connally sat next to her husband. Ahead of them sat the driver and another Secret Service man.

A limousine filled with Secret Service agents drove behind the president's. Vice President Johnson and Mrs. Johnson rode in the third car, which was also accompanied by Secret Service men.

Large groups of cheering people lined the streets of Dallas as the motorcade moved along. Everything seemed to be in order on this bright, sunny fall day.

The President is Shot

At 12:30 P.M., the motorcade approached an expressway as it entered on the last leg of its trip. Without warning, a number of shots rang out. Kennedy was hit by two of the shots—one to his neck, the other to his head. A shot also struck Connally in the back. Some experts believe that the shot that struck Connally had first hit the president.

As the president slumped down in his seat with his head in his wife's lap, the limousine sped to nearby Parkland Hospital. Doctors worked desperately to save the life of the president. Sadly, Kennedy never regained consciousness and was pronounced dead at 1:00 P.M.

Doctors indicated that the president had no chance of survival because of his wounds. Governor Connally eventually recovered.

Vice President Johnson had been taken to the same hospital as Kennedy and Connally and remained there until the president died. Within minutes after Kennedy died, the vice president, Mrs. Johnson, Mrs. Kennedy, and the body of the late president were on their way to the airport where the presidential plane waited.

At 2:40 P.M., U.S. Federal District Court Judge Sarah T. Hughes administered the oath of office to Johnson, making him the thirty-sixth president of the United States.

▶ News Shocks the World

Within minutes of Kennedy's death, television and radio flashed the news of the shooting around the world. The biggest question that had to be answered was, "Who shot the president?"

Moments after the shooting, witnesses told authorities that the shots they heard came from the sixth floor window of the Texas School Book Depository. The building was on the route of the motorcade.

A search of the building found no killer, but they did find a rifle near a window. Police then continued their

▲ Johnson taking the oath of office onboard Air Force One. A newly widowed Jacqueline Kennedy stands to his left.

search until they learned that an employee of the building, Lee Harvey Oswald, had left the scene moments after the shooting.

At about 1:15 P.M., Oswald was said to have shot Dallas policeman J. D. Tippit while resisting arrest. A short time later, Oswald was found and arrested in a theater. He was taken to jail and was charged with killing President Kennedy and Officer Tippit.

For two days, police questioned Oswald about the murders. Oswald continually denied having anything to do with either of them.

On Sunday, November 24, with a nation watching the funeral proceedings of the late president, Oswald was shot and killed while being taken from the Dallas city jail to the county jail. Jack Ruby, a Dallas nightclub owner, shot Oswald as most of the country watched on television.

Oswald was taken to the same hospital President Kennedy had died in. Oswald died forty-eight hours after Kennedy's death.

Kennedy Remembered

President John F. Kennedy, who had captured the nation's attention with his "New Frontier" program, was dead.

From the moment it was announced that Kennedy had been shot, television and radio stations around the United States stopped regular broadcasting and devoted all of their airtime to covering the fallen leader's funeral. From the mid-afternoon hours of November 22 until the end of his funeral on November 25, the United States'—and rest of the world's—focus was on Kennedy.

Kennedy's body had been brought back to the White House and placed in the East Room for twenty-four hours. On November 24, the president's flag-draped coffin was carried to the Capitol Rotunda to lie in state. Throughout the day and night, thousands of mourners passed by the guarded casket.

Jacqueline planned the funeral. She had studied President Abraham Lincoln's funeral. She arranged her husband's funeral, following many of the same rituals that had been done for Lincoln.[1]

Throughout the entire ordeal, Mrs. Kennedy maintained her composure. She vowed she would conduct herself in a manner that would have made her husband proud. She spoke of arranging a dignified but impressive funeral that was simple, yet befitted the high office of the presidency. She wanted the kind of funeral she thought her husband would have approved of.[2]

Not since the royal funeral of King Edward VII in 1910 had the world seen such a gathering as President Kennedy's funeral on November 25. Over ninety countries were represented at the funeral. There were 220 foreign chiefs of state, heads of government, members of royal families, and leading foreign dignitaries coming to Washington, D.C., to pay their last respects. Included in the group were Irish President Eamon de Valera, French President Charles de Gaulle, Belgian King Baudouin, Ethiopian Emperor Haile Selassie, Philippine President Diosdado Macapagal, and West German President Heinrich Luebke.

▲ Jacqueline Kennedy gazed at her husband's casket and grasped the hands of her two small children as she left the church.

▶ Kennedy Burial

As the Kennedy casket was carried into the bright sunlight, Mrs. Kennedy paused momentarily on the steps of the church with her children, Caroline and John, Jr., at her side. As he watched his father's casket being brought down the steps, John, Jr., saluted.

This was the last time the family of President Kennedy gathered for him. Included in the procession were his mother, brothers and sisters, brothers-in-law and sisters-in-law, and other relatives (Jack's father, Joseph, Sr., was at home recovering from a stroke suffered earlier).

At 3:34 P.M. on November 25, Kennedy was buried with full military honors at Arlington National Cemetery.[3]

▲ *Millions of visitors have come to Arlington National Cemetery to pay their respects to President Kennedy.*

An eternal flame was lit by Mrs. Kennedy to burn over the president's grave.

Kennedy Name Lives On

Since Kennedy's death, millions of visitors have come to his grave to pay their respects. John F. Kennedy's life, death, and the Kennedy family are still topics of interest that gain media attention. His story book romance with Jacqueline Bouvier was called "Camelot" by the press. The glamorous relationship helped make Kennedy one of the most popular presidents ever.

The fifty-cent coin was minted in the United States with the likeness of Kennedy on it, replacing that of Benjamin Franklin. A stamp honoring the fallen president was also produced for use in the United States.

Since his death in 1963, many public buildings, roadways, and other geographical sites throughout the world have been named for President Kennedy. In 1964, President Johnson renamed the NASA installation in Florida the Kennedy Space Center. In 1979, the John Fitzgerald Kennedy Library and Museum was opened in Boston, Massachusetts.

Controversy Over the Assassination

There have been many different theories as to how the president was assassinated. While some believe that Oswald was the lone killer, there are others who think there was a conspiracy to kill the president.

In 1964, the Warren Commission, headed by Chief Justice of the Supreme Court Earl Warren, was formed to investigate the assassination. Later that same year, the commission concluded that Oswald had acted alone.

Those findings did not drive away the doubts that surrounded the assassination. In the 1970s, a special committee of the United States House of Representatives reexamined the evidence surrounding Kennedy's assassination. That committee accepted the testimony of experts who claimed shots were fired from two locations along the president's motorcade at the same time. In 1978, the committee concluded that Kennedy "was probably assassinated as a result of a conspiracy."[4]

Since that time, other authorities and organizations have disputed the committee's conclusions. To this day, speculation about what really happened and who was responsible continues.

Chapter Notes

Chapter 1. Military Hero, August 1943

1. Richard Tregaskis, *John F. Kennedy and PT–109* (New York: Random House, 1962) p. 103.

2. Ibid., p. 107.

3. *John F. Kennedy: A Personal Story* (A&E Television Networks, Biography), 1997, videocassette.

4. Tregaskis, p. 117.

5. H. William Heller, "The Military Years," *Kennedy Galleries: Florida International Museum,* n.d., <http://www.floridamuseum.org/main%20tguide.html> (February 14, 2002).

6. *John F. Kennedy: A Personal Story,* videocassette.

Chapter 2. Early Years, 1917–1945

1. *John F. Kennedy: A Personal Story* (A&E Television Networks, Biography), 1997, videocassette.

2. Ibid.

3. Biography Resource Center: Gale Group, "Kennedy, Joseph P(atrick)," *Biography.com,* 2001, <http://search.biography.com/print_record.pl?id=16492> (February 14, 2002).

4. Ibid.

5. *John F. Kennedy: A Personal Story,* videocassette.

6. David C. Whitney, *The American Presidents* (Doubleday & Company, 1985), p. 305.

Chapter 3. Kennedy in Congress, 1946–1959

1. *The New York Times* Company, "Death of Brother in War Thrust Kennedy Into Career of Politics," *The New York Times on the Web: On This Day, November 23, 1963, 2000,* http://www.nytimes.com/learning/general/onthisday/bday/0529e.html> (February 14, 2002).

2. Doug Levy, "*USA Today*, September 13, 1996," *Presidential Exhibit Reviews*, n.d., <www.collphyphil.org/gallrvws.htm> (February 14, 2002).

Chapter 4. A Popular President, 1960–1963

1. *Time Magazine*, "1960 Kennedy-Nixon," *Moments in Time: The Presidential Debates*, 2000, <http://www.time.com/time/campaign2000/debates/photoalbum/photo_01.html> (February 14, 2002).

2. David C. Whitney, *The American Presidents* (Doubleday & Company, Inc., 1985), pp. 308–309.

3. Hugh Sidey, *John F. Kennedy: President* (New York: 1963), p. 188.

Chapter 5. A Fatal Trip, November 1963

1. H. William Heller, "The Military Years," *Kennedy Galleries: Florida International Museum*, n.d., <http://www.floridamuseum.org/main%20tguide.html> (February 14, 2002), p. 26.

Chapter 6. Kennedy Remembered

1. Associated Press, *The Torch is Passed: The Associated Press Story of the Death of a President* (New York: The Associated Press, 1963), p. 31.

2. Ibid., p. 29.

3. Ibid., p. 96.

4. United States Government Printing Office, "Report of the Select Committee on Assassinations of the U.S. House of Representatives," *National Archives and Records Administration*, 1979, reprinted online in 2001, <http://www.nara.gov/research/jfk/hscaic.html> (February 14, 2002).

Further Reading

Anderson, Catherine C. *Jacqueline Kennedy Onassis: Woman of Courage.* Minneapolis, Minn.: The Lerner Publishing Group, 1995.

Burerer, David. *John F. Kennedy and a New Generation.* Glenview, Ill.: Scott, Foresman/Little, Brown College Division, 1988.

Freedman, Lawrence. *Kennedy's Wars: Berlin, Cuba, Laos, & Vietnam.* New York: Oxford University Press, Inc., 2000.

Giglio, James N. *The Presidency of John F. Kennedy.* Lawrence: University Press of Kansas, 1991.

Gow, Catherine. *The Cuban Missile Crisis.* San Diego, Calif.: Lucent Books, 1997.

Griffiths, John. *Cuban Missile Crisis.* Vero Beach, Fla.: Rourke Enterprises, Inc., 1987.

Harrison, Barbara G. and David Terris. *A Twilight Struggle: The Life of John Fitzgerald Kennedy.* New York: Lothrop, Lee & Shepard Books, 1992.

Joseph, Paul. *John F. Kennedy.* Edina, Minn.: ABDO Publishing Company, 2000.

Klein, Edward. *All Too Human: The Love Story of Jack and Jackie Kennedy.* New York: Pocket Books, 1996.

Landman, Susan. *A History Mystery: Who Shot JFK?* New York: Morrow Avon, 1992.

Spies, Karen Borneman. *John F. Kennedy.* Berkeley Heights, N.J.: Enslow Publishers, Inc., 1999.

Waggoner, Jeffrey. *The Assassination of President Kennedy: Opposing Viewpoints.* San Diego, Calif.: Greenhaven Press, Inc., 1989.

$19.95

DATE			